THE COYOTE'S HEART

A 33-DAY DEVOTIONAL FOR YOUNG MEN

T.J. GREANEY

founder of Kids Outdoor Zone

KOZ
Publishing
Company
KidsOutdoorZone.com

All Scripture is from the THE HOLY BIBLE, NEW INTERNATIONAL VERSION®, NIV® Copyright © 1973, 1978, 1984, 2011 by Biblica, Inc.® Used by permission. All rights reserved worldwide.

The scripture marked AMP is taken from the AMPLIFIED BIBLE (AMP): Scripture taken from the AMPLIFIED® BIBLE, Copyright © 1954, 1958, 1962, 1964, 1965, 1987 by the LockmanFoundation Used by Permission. (www.Lockman.org)

Cover and interior design: TLC Book Design, TLCBookDesign.com

Coyote photo: actionsports. Image from Bigstock.com.

ISBN: 979-8-9871434-0-7 (paperback)

First Edition

This book is dedicated to the first guys who
went on a KOZ outing with me: Josh, Wayne, and Travis.
And to my absolute Ride and Die posse: Darius, Christian,
Kyle, and Jon-Michael. You guys have given me
a big part of the adventure heart I longed for.
I am so proud of you and who you have become.
KEEP CLIMBING AND CHASING JESUS.

CONTENTS

Even youths grow weary and tired,

And vigorous young men stumble badly,

But those who wait for the Lord,

Will gain new strength and renew their power;

They will lift up their wings [and rise up close to God] like eagles,

They will run and not become weary,

They will walk and not grow tired.

ISAIAH 40:30-31

(Amplified Bible, AMP)

INTRODUCTION

A coyote is a special, wild, and fierce creature. When I sit out on my farm in the evenings I can hear them, close and far, barking, yelping, and talking to each other. I see their tracks on the sandy trails and roads. I imagine them running, playing, hunting, chasing each other.

The native Indians in America had a lot of stories about them, both good and bad. Many Indian nations believe that seeing them brings joy and happiness. Some Native American tribes believe that a close encounter with a coyote brings happiness into the life of a person who sees it. They believed that coyotes were encouraging them before battles.

Being a guy can be hard. Making good choices and decisions can be confusing and difficult. Learning to make good decisions requires us to be trained. We need good advice. We need someone to teach us how to make decisions, how to make good choices, how to be a good man.

The Coyote's Heart has 33 different topics that a guy is faced with during his life. These are real stories and experiences like the ones you will have. Take this time to read each topic or look up the ones that you need answers for, maybe share them with a friend who needs some help.

I include scriptures that teach us how to navigate each of these topics. God knew what we needed and gave us great counsel and advice in the Bible on how to live life well. And, of course, prayer is huge and everything we do needs some prayer. Praying is just a conversation with God and doesn't have to be fancy. There is a prayer for each topic.

A coyote is smart, fearless, and strong. He loves his friends and family. He will fight for them, run to them when they need help, and never leave them behind. You have the heart of a coyote.

He loves you.
Now go **DO HARD THINGS!**

– TJ

False Evidence Appearing Real

I haven't had anything bad happen in the dark, but I am not sure why it can still be a scary place for me. Fear can be about more than a dark closet or nighttime in the woods. Fear can be of losing someone, fear of the unknown, fear that something might or might not happen.

Fear is a real feeling when it is in the right place. Fear of falling, hurting yourself, a creepy person walking toward you. God gave us fear to protect us.

Fear can also be used by Satan to create all kinds of crummy things in our life. He does not want you to be strong in your faith and smart in your choices. He will use things like fear of going to church or youth group because of what some people might say.

When we have Jesus in our hearts, we have the Holy Spirit. The Holy Spirit is here to help us navigate our lives and make choices that don't include allowing fear to guide us.

PRAYER

*Lord, thank You for caring about me. Lord, I pray against the bad way
fear is used and ask You to give me a brave and fearless heart.
I want to live for You, Jesus. Amen*

SCRIPTURE

Isaiah 43:1
"Don't fear, for I have redeemed you;
I have called you by name; you are Mine."

TRAILHEAD

Tell yourself every day, even several times a day if you need to:
"I am not afraid, I have Jesus." Write down some things you will
pray about not being afraid of.

GIRLS

Girls can be the best and worst thing ever—I say that being funny. You might not understand that today, but you will. One thing that is true, forever, no matter what, you have to treat them with kindness and courtesy.

It doesn't matter what the reason is or how frustrated you might get, a boy must never hit, push, or be physically mean to a girl, ever. This is a solid guy rule you should never break.

A guy should also always open the door for a girl. Walk to her side of the car and open the door for her; open any door for her to walk in ahead of you. Always get up and offer your seat and always walk on the street side of the sidewalk when walking with a girl. If you follow these rules, one day you will feel like a hero, because you are.

PRAYER
Lord, thank You for girls. Thank You for the gift they are.
Lord, please help me to always be mindful of them. Help me to always be
a gentleman, kind, and know You have me here to protect and care for
the girls You put in my life. That includes my mom and sisters first.

SCRIPTURE
Proverbs 3:15
"She is more precious than jewels,
and nothing you desire can compare with her."

TRAILHEAD
Think about the girls and ladies in your life. Get in the habit of opening doors, saying, "Yes Ma'am," and helping when they need help.
You will feel great and so will they. Write down some girls' or ladies' names in your life who deserve respect.

TRAIL NOTES

BRAVERY

I dream of fighting the bad guys. Drawing a sword and fighting off the beast and knights from the dark side. I dream of running into a burning building and rescuing a family and their dog. Flying a fighter jet, becoming a Navy Seal. Every guy dreams of being brave and fierce. We are made for it.

Bravery is telling an adult if someone is being a bully. Being brave can be trying out for a play or sports. It can be telling an adult the truth when you know you are going to get into trouble, but you do it anyway. Deep inside, all of us want to be brave and honest.

PRAYER

Lord, thank You for today. I pray, Jesus, that I can be an example of bravery to others. Use me, Jesus, to help others. Help me know when to be brave, when You want me to stand firm, and how to overcome anything that gets in Your way for me.

SCRIPTURE

Deuteronomy 31:6
"Be strong and courageous. Do not fear or be in dread of them,
for it is the Lord your God who goes with you.
He will not leave you or forsake you."

TRAILHEAD

Ask Jesus, "Where do I need to be brave today?"
You may have to think about it for a while, but God will tell you.
Just ask every day, and listen closely. What did God say to you
about being brave?

TRAIL NOTES

OVERCOMING

There will always be things, hard things, that you are going to have to overcome. I remember when I was young, my dog was hit by a car. That day he was with me; ran into the street and was hit. He did not make it. It was my fault.

I was so upset. I cried a lot. I didn't understand why God let that happen. To top it off my mom and dad didn't seem to care. They made me pay the bill. I just couldn't figure any of it out.

It took time to overcome that day. Eventually I didn't think about it much as the hurt faded and life got back to normal. Yes, things like that can seem like they could never get better. Minutes seemed like days. Overcoming your parents' divorce, your dad leaving, someone getting sick or dying, a girl breaking up with you, or a good buddy snubbing you can hurt. It just does. But time and God will get you through it. It really does get better.

PRAYER

Jesus, please give me the strength to overcome my hurting right now.
God, it is hard for me to understand and see the end of the hurt.
I have to trust You today, God, because it is hard to believe in
anything else and I need You. Amen

SCRIPTURE

Isaiah 41:13
"For I am the LORD your God who takes hold of your right hand
and says to you, 'Do not fear; I will help you.'"

TRAILHEAD

Today look for ways to help someone else. Does somebody need their yard mowed? Do you know a little kid who needs someone to hang out with, walk to the park, throw the ball with them? Do you know an older person who needs some help? Overcome your hurt by giving back. Find an adult you can trust and talk to them about what you are feeling. Your feelings are real, they matter. Write down what you need to overcome.

KINDNESS

How do you feel when someone is nice to you? It feels so good.

I remember my wife telling me about one day at the grocery store when she smiled at an older fellow and said, "Good morning." He smiled the biggest smile. She said when she left the store, they saw each other again and he stopped her and said, "Thank you. I am having a hard day and your kindness made my day better." Wow, just a smile and saying "good morning" is all it takes sometimes!

Kindness makes our hearts feel really good.

PRAYER

Jesus, thank You for being kind to me. Thank You for the people who are kind to me. Lord, help me to be kind to others today.

SCRIPTURE

Colossians 3:12

"Therefore, as God's chosen people, holy and dearly loved, clothe yourselves with compassion, kindness, humility, gentleness, and patience."

TRAILHEAD

Who is it you need to be kind to? What if you try your best to smile and say hi to everyone you can? Write down what happened when you were kind all day.

FRIENDSHIP

There is nothing like a good friend. When I was a kid, my first best friend was Roy Newman. He lived next door and was the first person I ever knew who was missing a finger. I don't know how it got cut off, but no matter, we were best friends. Roy and I did everything together.

Adventures in the bayous and woods by our house were epic. We hunted for frogs and snakes and everything wild. We told stories and ate over at each other's houses. Then one day he told me he was moving and the next thing I knew, he was gone. It was hard. But I got new friends and life kept going. Friendship is kindness to other people and doing life with them.

PRAYER

Jesus, thank You for my friends. Jesus, I need a good friend.
Lord, help me to be the kind of friend that makes You smile, is helpful and kind. I pray I have the kind of friends who like to do the right things.
Jesus, please keep me away from those who are a bad influence or tempt me to do things I know I should not do. Thanks for being my friend, Jesus, and help me be a good friend to others. Amen

SCRIPTURE

Proverbs 12:26
"The righteous choose their friends carefully,
but the way of the wicked leads them astray."

TRAILHEAD

Who are my friends? Do I owe a friend an apology?
What are some things I can do to be a better friend today?
Is there someone who doesn't have a friend I can try to be
a friend to today? Write some names down.

TRAIL NOTES

BULLY

We had two really mean bullies when I was in middle school. I don't know why they decided I was one of the people they needed to be mean to, but they did. It was terrible to go to school and always have to worry about when they would decide to pick on me. Adults can be bullies too.

I have never been a bully. I always want to help people who are getting treated badly by someone. Some people tell you that punching a bully in the nose works—maybe. I think you have to find an adult you trust. You should also watch out for others like little kids, your brothers and sisters, and even adults. If you see them being bullied, you have to tell another adult.

PRAYER
Jesus, thank You for being in my life today. I pray for strength and wisdom in how I handle bullies and mean people. Jesus, put adults in my life to help answer the questions and and help me know what I can do. Jesus, show me someone I can help who feels like I do. I know when I help others, I feel better, stronger, and closer to You. Amen

SCRIPTURE
Matthew 5:44
"But I say to you, 'Love your enemies and pray for those who persecute you, so that you may be sons of your Father who is in heaven.'"

TRAILHEAD
Look for someone sitting alone. Someone who needs to hear an encouraging word. Say hi, ask how they are. Smile at them. If you see someone being bullied, step in. Tell an adult. Don't be the guy who sees it happen but walks away. Maybe you bullied someone and need to ask them to forgive you. Who can you go to if you feel bullied? Write down some safe names.

HAPPINESS

My dog makes me happy. Sometimes he does dumb things and I get mad, but he really does make me happy. My friends make me happy.

I find if I spend a lot of time in social media or watching scary or depressing movies or television too much, I can feel bad. If you want to be happy—feel happy—you have to put yourself in the "happy seat." This may seem funny but do something you did when you were little that made you happy. Be around positive and happy people as much as you can. Happiness really does rub off on you when you are around happy people.

PRAYER

Jesus, I love to laugh. I love funny things and the feeling I get when I am happy. Some days I don't want to be happy, or I just don't feel happy. I know everyone has their ups and downs but today, Jesus, I am asking You to help me see You, feel the happiness and joy that You give us. Lord, help me laugh and smile at someone today. Let me feel the happiness I long for. Amen

SCRIPTURE

Psalm 16:11

"You make known to me the path of life; in your presence there is fullness of joy; at your right hand are pleasures forevermore."

TRAILHEAD

When you get up in the mornings you need to tell yourself, "I am happy, I like myself, this is going to be a good day." Then plan on doing something that makes you happy. A bag of candy, a silly movie, hanging with a funny friend. We really can choose happiness and joy. Sometimes it takes some work, but you can do it. Learn a good joke and tell it to someone, help someone else be happy today too. Write down what makes you happy today.

TRAIL NOTES

FAMILY

My parents divorced when I was 13 and that was it. My family broke up. It was hard. When my family was together, we did things like camping, fishing, playing in the yard at home together. Everyone wants a loving family. Everyone. If your family is all together, then tell God thank you every day.

Lots of families split, parents divorce or pass away. Brothers and sisters get separated from us. We can be really mad because our parents get a divorce. That doesn't mean Jesus left you. Life will always have its ups and downs. You'll have hard days. But one day you will be the decision-maker on how you want your family to be. You can be the kind, gentle, loving parent. You can teach your kids about Jesus and enjoy being together.

PRAYER

Jesus, please protect our family. Watch over them and keep them safe. Lord, I know You care about me. Help me to appreciate my family together or apart. Jesus, help me to see the good in my family. Help me to be a loving example to others around me. Lord, if there is someone who is hurting because their family life is hard right now, show me who they are so I can help. Amen

SCRIPTURE

Genesis 2:24

"Therefore a man shall leave his father and his mother and hold fast to his wife, and they shall become one flesh."

TRAILHEAD

Divorce and not seeing one of your parents may be the hardest thing in your life ever. This week write a letter, note, or a card to a person in your family. Not an email or text. Hand-deliver it or mail it. Go for a walk with a family member. Ask them what they like, what makes them happy. Do something fun with a little brother or sister. We all long for family, everyone does. Pray for your family, grandparents, even if you don't see them or even know them. God knows your heart. Write down who needs prayer in your family right now.

BROTHERS

If you don't have a brother, the closest thing would be a very best friend. I grew up with two brothers, a younger and older. I remember following my older brother around everywhere he went. Sometimes he let me, other times he and his friends ditched.

We had go-carts and bikes and played in the woods a lot. We caught turtles, lizards, and frogs. We climbed trees and built forts and camp sites. We spent a lot of time outdoors and we loved it.

Eventually my parents divorced, and I ran away. I was alone. Thinking back now, it was sad. We should never be all alone. My brothers and I talked some. Not always, because we were not together. As we got older, we got to see each other more and we do some amazing things together to this day.

If you don't have brothers, it's okay. Your close friends will be your brothers. If you are not close with your brothers, pray for them; God does amazing things when we pray for people. Brothers and sisters should always be there for each other.

PRAYER

Jesus, thank You for my brothers (friend). Please protect them and care for them. Keep us close Lord and help me be the brother (friend) I really want to be. Amen

SCRIPTURE

Romans 12:10
"Love one another with brotherly affection.
Outdo one another in showing honor."

TRAILHEAD

So what could your brother (friend) do for you that would make you happy? Do that for them. Don't make a big deal of it, just do something nice you know they will like. Brothers (friends) forever. Write your brothers' names and friends who are close like a brother so you remember to pray for them.

SISTERS

My sisters were really cool. They were both younger than me, but it was great to have sisters. They loved to do girl things and I benefitted from learning how to cook and bake from them. Yes, we argued and sometimes were mad at each other, but that happens in every family.

Learning how to treat a girl is important and it starts with your sister(s) if you have one. There were times I felt like I needed to watch out for them, make sure they were safe. That is something a brother does.

If you have a sister, you are blessed. If you don't, read this prayer because it will help you pick a girlfriend and a wife one day.

PRAYER
Lord, thank You for sisters. Thank You for all the things they teach us.
Lord, please watch over my sisters. Watch over my friends' sisters, Jesus.
Lord, I always want to be a guy who is polite, strong, and caring. Help me be
that way with my sisters and all the ladies, girls, in my life. Amen

SCRIPTURE
1 Timothy 5:2
"Older women as mothers, younger women as sisters, in all purity."

TRAILHEAD
Sisters are a real gift. Be the brother your sister needs. Strong guys
are always polite and caring. They stand up and offer their seat to
their sister. They open and hold the door for them too.
Be kind and helpful with your sister, a girl, or lady today. You feel
great when you are caring. Write down your sisters' names and
girls who are close like a sister you can pray for.

PARENTS

My wife and I have done pretty well as parents. We worked really hard to stay together, teach our kids about Jesus. We taught them about working hard, caring for each other. Being a parent is the toughest job you can have. We know we messed up plenty of times, but we prayed and still pray every day to be the best parents we can be. You get to choose if you want to be a parent, and if you do, you can be awesome.

PRAYER

Lord, thank You for my parents. Lord, I pray that today is a good day,
a day they can have it easy as a parent. I pray for them to be healthy,
to have good friends, to laugh, and to know You are close by.
Thank You for teaching them to be parents. Amen

SCRIPTURE

Ephesians 6:1–3

"Children, obey your parents in the Lord, for this is right.
Honor your father and mother (this is the first commandment with
a promise), that it may go well with you and that you may
live long in the land."

TRAILHEAD

Be kind to your parents today. Even if they are not together,
that is hard for them too. Call them, tell them thanks for being a parent.
Tell them you know being a parent some days can be hard and
that you love them. If one of your parents is not living anymore,
write them a letter.

Think about all the things you will do if you are a parent one day.
God teaches us what to do and how to be a good parent.
Write down things you will do as a parent.

ADVENTURE

I love adventure. All guys do; not all guys get to. When I was a kid, we had small patches of trees all around our house. We explored there all the time. We tried fishing in every place that had water. We climbed every tree. We built forts in the living room, in the back yard, in the trees, and by the lake. One time I was walking along a trail and tried to take a short cut and slid on some loose rocks. I cut my hands up pretty good. But I learned some important lessons that day. Watch where you walk, stay on the trail, be careful of loose rocks. Simple lessons learned the hard way.

PRAYER
Lord, thank You for having a heart for adventure.
I can feel it when I see others on an adventure. I know You made me
that way. Help me to find adventure in my life. Help me to know which
trails to take and which ones not to take. Thanks for the outdoors, Jesus.
Help me be strong outside. Amen

SCRIPTURE
Luke 1:37
"For nothing will be impossible with God."

TRAILHEAD
It's easy to sit and stare at videos watching other people do cool things.
Every guy needs to get outside and have adventure. Find a friend,
get on your bike and ride. Go for a walk, turn it into a hike.
Camp out in your backyard to learn how to camp and survive outside.
Join a club or group that does cool stuff outside. A lot of guys don't
know it, but you really do need to explore something cool outdoors.
Adventure makes you smarter, stronger, braver, and guess what,
Jesus is there.
Write three adventures you would like to have one day.

DANGER

Sometimes we do the wrong thing for the wrong reason, and it can be dangerous. I was playing with gas one time and it blew up in my face burning all the hair and my skin. I was lucky. Being a fighter jet pilot can be dangerous, but for the right reasons. Most of the time when we are about to do something dangerous, we know it. Danger is real. People can get hurt, even die. Danger is serious.

PRAYER

Lord, I don't want to make stupid choices; help me to be smart.
Help me to hear You when I am getting close to something dangerous.
Lord, help me to be "dangerous for good." Amen

SCRIPTURE

Proverbs 27:12
"The prudent sees danger and hides himself,
but the simple go on and suffer for it."

TRAILHEAD

Think first. Stop and think. You are an incredibly smart person; think before you do something that is dangerous. If you have a friend doing something dangerous, try to help them stop. Tell a trusted adult if you have to. Satan likes to get us into dangerous places and to do dangerous things. Be smart, stop and think, a life might depend on it.
What was something dangerous in your life recently?
Write it down and remember it.

CHOICES

Chocolate or vanilla? Hamburger or hotdog? These are choices that are pretty easy to make. The hard choices can be: Do I hang out with this kid; should I tell the truth; I know my mom warned me about this but do I do it anyway. The choices you make say a lot about you. I remember once getting into trouble, bad trouble. Years later I had someone say something about it and I was embarrassed. I knew better at the time but did it anyway. I wish I had had someone to teach me how to make better decisions. I knew in my heart some decisions I was making were wrong, but I just wasn't strong enough to say, "No!"

PRAYER
Jesus, I want to make good choices. I know what they are but sometimes it is hard. Help me listen to You, Jesus, and not Satan and his dumb choices. Jesus, help me be a good example to others with the choices I make.

SCRIPTURE
Proverbs 3:5–6
"Trust in the Lord with all your heart, and do not lean on your own understanding. In all your ways acknowledge him, and he will make straight your paths."

TRAILHEAD
Making good choices will determine a whole lot of things in your life.
Some of your choices can stay with you your whole life.
You need to be careful, pray, and think about decisions that matter.
It can be hard, but with Jesus by your side, you got this!
Write some serious decisions you have to make.
Also write down your favorite: french fries or ice cream.

TROUBLE

"Hello, Trouble, where have you been? I have been waiting on you." That quote is from a knife commercial from years ago. I just don't like telling boys basically they'll be ready for trouble if they have a knife. Sometimes when a cowboy is working a horse and the rope gets twisted around his hand and a pole, he has to cut the rope fast. He was ready for trouble if he had his knife there. It maybe kept him from losing a finger or his hand.

When my parents divorced, I had a lot of trouble. When hard things happened, I didn't know what to do or who to talk to. I really needed someone to help me figure things out. Trouble is going to come. Being ready for it makes all the difference. It's not always a tool, it can be a person.

PRAYER

Jesus, I have trouble right now and I want to tell You myself.
Please protect me (protect my family, my friends, teachers). I have times
when I am scared, angry, worried, and confused. But I know You are
with me, Jesus, and I just want to tell You myself about the troubles
and ask for You to help me know what to do.
I need Your help, Jesus, most of all. Amen

SCRIPTURE

Nahum 1:7
"The Lord is good, a stronghold in the day of trouble; he knows those who take refuge in him."

TRAILHEAD

The first thing when trouble comes is to pray. If you know Jesus, you need to talk to Him. Tell Him about the trouble and ask for Him to be there with you. The storm might not pass right away, your parents may still get a divorce, your car may not get fixed. Jesus is not a wish-and-get-it god. He is like a best friend who will be there with you and help when He can. He really does love you. That is worth everything. Write out a place or thing where you are having trouble.

SCHOOL

There is so much about school that is important. Of course, it is where we learn math and reading and science. Some people do sports or FFA, science club, or theatre. We also meet most of our friends there and learn how to deal with other people and situations in our life. Even homeschool is a place we learn more than just school studies. I didn't do well in school and looking back now I wish I had. School is important and you need to make an effort to do well, maybe do great. It can be hard, but few important and great things come easy.

PRAYER

Lord, thank You for school. I know I don't feel like saying thank you, but I know I need to. Jesus, help me to be focused, polite, kind, thoughtful at school. Lord, keep Satan and the bad influences, the distractions, and the trouble away from me every day at school. Help me be bold and not afraid to let people know about You and how You have helped me. Thank You, Jesus. Amen

SCRIPTURE

Proverbs 2:6
"For the Lord gives wisdom;
from his mouth come knowledge and understanding."

TRAILHEAD

It can be hard to see what is important about school when you are young. Sometimes you have to trust the adults around you when they tell you, "Be strong, finish." There are a handful of things that make a big difference when you are an adult; one of them is finishing school well. Sometimes you have to "do hard things." You are smart, brave, and can do this—be strong. Write down some of the hard things about school.

MOM

I was lucky, my mom liked to cook. We never ate out, she always made something for dinner. I loved my mom's cooking. When I was growing up and started getting into trouble, I did not respect her or what she asked me to do. It makes me sad today to think about how I treated her sometimes. She told me later she always prayed for me, all the time. You only get one mom—treat her with the respect and honor she deserves. If your mom was not a good mom, it could be she had a lot of hard things happen to her when she was young. Sometimes you have to be strong for your mom, help her, pray for her.

PRAYER

Jesus, I want to ask for You to watch over my mom.
I know she works hard and does the best she can. I know she loves me
like only a mom can. I want to ask for You to give her an extra amount
of joy and happiness. Let her know You are with her, Jesus.
I love my mom. Amen

SCRIPTURE

Exodus 20:12
"Honor your father and your mother, that your days may be long
in the land that the Lord your God is giving you."

TRAILHEAD

It's your turn to give it up and pray for your mom. Do the things
she asks you to do. If she says put the video games away and take out
the trash, jump up and do it. Don't talk back to her, don't make
life harder on her. You can be a big help. You should be.
Write down five things you can do better to help your mom.

EXERCISE

Some guys love sports and do everything they can at school. I never played sports in school. No basketball, football, or anything. I remember once in the 4th grade they had everyone outside for a race. I don't know why the whole 4th grade needed to race but we did. I won that race, and I was so happy. I think that is why I love to run and hike today. There are a lot of things that can be new for us, and maybe exercise is one. I want you to know it can help you in a lot of ways. You do not have to be the leader of the football team, or a player on the championship team. But you do have to move your body. Drop the phone and take the challenge to hike, join a sport, get on your bike. Do it for you!

PRAYER

Jesus, help me to take care of my body. I know I will feel better if I exercise, but sometimes doing what I should do can be hard for me. Give me energy. I pray to find a friend who loves to do these things. Help me, Jesus. Thank You for giving me this incredible body, Lord. It is powerful and strong. Amen

SCRIPTURE

1 Corinthians 6:19–20

"Or do you not know that your body is a temple of the Holy Spirit within you, whom you have from God? You are not your own, for you were bought with a price. So glorify God in your body."

TRAILHEAD

Whenever I feel overwhelmed, anxious, mad, sad, or lonely, I go outside and go for a walk or a run. I pick up a shovel and dig a hole. I use my hammer to build something. Our bodies need exercise. Our body is connected to our mind and how we feel in our heads. It is so bad for us to sit inside staring at a screen hour after hour. You know what we say, "Do hard things." Get moving! Write three ways you exercise or could move your body and make it healthier.

BIBLE

When I was growing up, I never knew anything about the Bible. I was an adult before someone shared with me the amazing things inside the Bible. Stories about a guy who killed a giant with a sling shot, a guy who fought a lion in a cave. I learned about Jesus and all the things He did, from curing people who were sick, teaching people how to live their lives well, to even raising a child from the dead. And then I learned what it really meant when I learned about how He died and why. All that and so much more inside the book I never read that was written for me! I have read a lot of books now and the Bible is always the one that amazes me the most. Thanks, Jesus, for Your book.

PRAYER

Jesus, thank You for your words in the Bible. Thank You for the stories before You came and after You died. Jesus, help me to understand the Bible. Help me to hear You speak when I read the Bible. Jesus, thank You for giving us this incredible way to live, written right there in the Bible. Amen

SCRIPTURE

Matthew 4:4

"But he answered, 'It is written, "Man shall not live by bread alone, but by every word that comes from the mouth of God.""'"

TRAILHEAD

Learning to read was a huge step for me. Some people love to read and read all the time; I had to learn. But I did and now reading the Bible is one of my favorite things. If you are reading this, you are doing great—good job! Write down two stories you know about in the Bible. Then go find them and write down where they are in the Bible.

TRAIL NOTES

JESUS SPEAKS

When I read the Bible I see that Jesus spoke. In some Bibles, His words are in red. I did not understand that He actually can speak to me though. The idea can be scary in some ways. You know when your friend or someone you know wants you to do something you know you should not do, and you hear that little voice in your head that says, "Don't do it"? That is the Holy Spirit, Jesus. When you have Him in your heart (Romans 10:9), He is there to help you and you can learn to hear Him like that. Reading your Bible is the first and most important way to learn to hear His voice. Read away, cowboy.

PRAYER

Jesus, I don't know if I understand hearing from You, but I want to know Your voice. I so want to be able to ask You questions and know Your will for me. Remove the things in the way of me hearing Your words Jesus. I love You. Amen

SCRIPTURE

Romans 10:17
"So faith comes from hearing, and hearing through the word of Christ."

TRAILHEAD

You can't hear well in a noisy room. Life sems so busy and so many people are constantly on their phones, staring at things on a screen. It is so important to learn to be in a quiet place. It's easier to hear God when you are quiet. Give yourself a break and drop the electronics and go for a walk. Look at the birds, the trees, the clouds. Write some things you would like to hear about from God.

TRAIL NOTES

CHURCH

I never really understood church when I was a kid. I mean, we went to a church, but I never felt a part of anything there. I didn't care. Then I visited a small church with a friend, and it was different. People there talked to each other, cared for each other. It felt like a family. There were some adults there who listened to me and were there for me. I loved it.

Church is a good thing. It is important to find one you like, but you need to have one and be a part of the youth group, boys' outings, and church on Sunday if you can. God loves us and cares about us and wants us together in a church, a church family. It's a good thing.

PRAYER
Jesus, thank You for churches. Thank You for my church.
Help me be a part of the church, Jesus. I want to get to know other guys
in church and learn what church has to offer. It can be hard sometimes,
Jesus, to get to church, but, Jesus, I pray You help me with all that
You have for me and being in a church. Amen

SCRIPTURE
Mathew 18:20
"For where two or three are gathered in my name,
there am I among them."

TRAILHEAD
Not everybody agrees that you need to go to church to be close to God.
In a lot of ways that can be true, but He really does want us together.
Learning from others, doing things together as a church family.
You can also be a part of helping other kids who need help.
You were there once, so go and help. Write out a few things
you like about church. If you don't have a church right now,
write what you would like in a church.

LIFE VERSE

Knowing what the Bible says is so important. One of the ways we can make the Bible real for us is to pray for one verse that fits who we are. Make it your verse, your life verse. Mine was Isaiah 40:29–31. It really made me feel like I could be strong, I could know who Jesus was, and even if I goofed up, I could keep going. Read it and see if you agree. Now I feel it has changed as I got older, as my life mission changed. Now it is Proverbs 22:6. Do you know that one? It is my life verse, but it is actually about you!

PRAYER

Jesus, please show me my life verse. I know You have something giant for my life and the Bible is Your words. I would love to have Your words be part of who I am every day. Show me the verse You have for me today, Lord. Amen

SCRIPTURE

Romans 15:4

"For whatever was written in former days was written for our instruction, that through endurance and through the encouragement of the Scriptures we might have hope."

TRAILHEAD

A life verse can be so powerful, and you should try to find which one is for you. Memorize it and know what it says before and after. Know what it means. Life is better with a life verse. Write down several verses and pray about them.

BEST FRIEND

They say a guy with a best friend is a lucky guy. I have some good friends, some really good friends and I have a best friend. We trust each other, we care for each other. If you have more than one friend, you are really lucky. The fact of the matter is guys need friends. Friendship works both ways. To be the best best friend, you have to call them, check on them, go to their house, do what they like as much as you want them to do what you like. You have to be a good friend if you want to have a best friend. A best friend is a real gift from God, and you need to make it important.

PRAYER

Jesus, thank You for my friendship with (name someone here).
I so want to be the best friend I can be to him. I know friendships
can be hard, but help me listen to him, pray for him, and be a
good influence for him. In Your name, Jesus. Amen

SCRIPTURE

John 15:13
"Greater love has no one than this, that someone
lay down his life for his friends."

TRAILHEAD

A best friend would die for his friend. That sounds crazy, but it's
what a soldier, a policeman, a fireman, and a hero does. It can be really
hard to be a best friend. You will only have a few of them your whole life.
You may have lots of friends, but only a few best friends. Thank God
for them. If you don't have a best friend—then pray for one!
Write down what you like about your best friend or what
you would like if you had a best friend.

MENTOR

Back in the old days, a dad or uncle or grandfather taught a boy how to do things. Run the tractor, milk a cow, build a fence. A mentor can also help you learn how to deal with personal things in your life. If there is trouble at home or school, your mentor can be there to talk with you.

I had a teacher once who was always nice to me. He tried really hard to help me. He was more than a teacher; he was a mentor. I remember the first time I went to church as a young teenager. I had not been to church in a long time and a guy came over and began talking to me. He always came and found me and taught me about the Bible. I will never forget him; he was a mentor. A mentor is someone who cares about you and deserves to be treated kindly.

PRAYER
Jesus, You walk with us and mentor us each day. Lots of times I don't hear You—teach me to hear. Jesus, also please put a mentor in my life to help me learn all the things a good, strong, fierce young man needs to know. Amen

SCRIPTURE
Psalm 32:8
"I will instruct you and teach you in the way you should go;
I will counsel you with my eye upon you."

TRAILHEAD
Every guy needs a mentor. You can be 10, 20, 30, 50, 60 years old, and still need a mentor. We never stop learning and never stop needing people in our lives who care about us and help us understand life. Pray for God to bring you a mentor, or if you have one, tell them thanks. Write down something you love about one of your mentors or that you want in a mentor when you find one.

DAD

I remember once when we were driving with my dad, we drove past a go-cart in a man's driveway. He stopped and talked to the man then bought the go-cart. Holy cow, this is great. We spent lots of weekends driving that crazy fast thing. We learned how to drive, work on a motor, use tools. It was one of the coolest things my dad ever did. Not because he bought it, but because he spent time with us.

My dad also drank too much, and it caused my parents to divorce. I was so mad and lonely for so long. I finally got to spend time with my dad again when I became an adult, and it got better but still hard.

Now I am a dad and I am so careful about not just being a good dad, but a great dad. Being a father is really important, and everyone deserves a good dad. A dad first loves Jesus, then loves his wife, then loves his kids. God made it that way.

PRAYER

Lord, I want to pray for my dad. I want to give him to You.
Lord, thank You for him and please give him the joy and life he deserves.
Keep him safe and healthy. Help my dad know You most of all Jesus. Amen

SCRIPTURE

Ephesians 6:4
"Fathers, do not provoke your children to anger,
but bring them up in the discipline and instruction of the Lord."

TRAILHEAD

If your dad is in your life, tell him thank you for being a dad who stayed
with his kids. If your dad is not in your life or you don't know him,
it will be okay. God helps us get through not having a dad in our life.
Be a part of a group with men, like Kids Outdoor Zone; they will
be there for you too. Not having a dad does not define who you are,
only God and you do. Write out the five best things a dad can do,
or a cool story about your dad.

OUTDOORS

When I was little, my family went camping. I am so blessed that we did–I love camping. I remember once when we were in a national park and it was dark. My sister said she had to go to the bathroom, and I was assigned to take her across the campground to the bathroom. We unzipped the tent and started walking. It was just light enough to see when all of a sudden a giant black bear walked in front of us. We turned and ran back to the tent as fast as we could. We were freaked out and scared! The bear walked across from our tent to another camp spot where the campers left all their food and ice chest on the picnic table. The bear began to eat everything that he could, and he didn't care who watched him. It was crazy.

PRAYER

Jesus, thank You for the outdoors. Help me learn to enjoy
Your amazing creation of clouds and animals, wind and rain.
Teach me how to hear You and see You there. I pray for others who
don't get to be outside. Help me show others the outdoors.
Thank You, Jesus, for this beautiful creation. Amen

SCRIPTURE

Genesis 1:26
"Then God said, 'Let us make man in our image, after our likeness.
And let them have dominion over the fish of the sea and over the birds
of the heavens and over the livestock and over all the earth and over
every creeping thing that creeps on the earth.'"

TRAILHEAD

I love the outdoors. You can see God outside better than anywhere else
I can think of. If you want to learn about peace, relaxing, smiling,
sweating, catching fish, hunting, camping, or hiking, you have to
get outside. While you are there, tell God hi. Write three outdoor
adventures you would like to take!

QUIET TIME

So much noise around us. So many people turn on noise the first thing they do when they get up—radio, TV, music. Then life is full of noise driving to school, people at school, school announcements. Then you add in watching things on your phone or computer. There is no real place to find quiet. Even when we do, we are so used to noise that we have a hard time with not having noise. If this is you, you are not alone. But it is in the quiet moments we hear God the best. We all need some God time and to hear what He has for us.

PRAYER

Jesus, help me be strong and find quiet moments to be with You.
Help me to not be anxious when things are quiet. Help me, Jesus,
to remember to rest my mind from all the noise and be still.
I am Yours Jesus, still my heart and mind. Amen

SCRIPTURE

John 10:27
"My sheep hear my voice,
and I know them, and they follow me."

TRAILHEAD

When you lie in bed tonight and before you fall asleep,
try to be still and quiet. No music, no TV. It might be hard with
noises around your house or outside, but lie there and tell Jesus
thank you for today and to give you peace and rest. Try walking a little
while one day, no noise, no headphones. Just you, quiet, and God.
It can be hard to learn, but it will be one of the most important things
you can do to take care of yourself and learn to hear God speak.
Write a question you have for God.

ANGELS

The Bible tells us about the good heavenly angels and the fallen angels that work for Satan. I know that the angels have protected me so many times. I don't think not falling off the mountain or not being struck by lightning was luck. Angels were protecting my son and me when we needed protection. One night on top of a mountain it stormed bad all night. Our little tent could barely handle it. That morning the clouds opened just long enough for us to get off the mountain. I believe in angels. I need them. (Read about fallen angels in the "Devil/Satan" section).

PRAYER

Jesus, I pray for Your angels to fill my room, walk with me,
beside me, in front of me. I know some people might not believe, but I do.
I know You sent them to protect us. Thank You for your angels, Jesus. Amen

SCRIPTURE

Psalm 91:11
"For he will command his angels concerning you
to guard you in all your ways."

TRAILHEAD

"I pray a hedge of heavenly warrior angels around our children tonight."
That is something my wife says every night. She prays that often.
I know angels have protected me. Write about a time
you think an angel has helped you.

DEVIL

There once was an angel who thought he was better than God. He thought he could run heaven and teach God a few things. Wrong. God threw him and all his buddies (fallen angels) out of heaven and down to earth—I wish he had picked somewhere else. There have been plenty of times I have made bad choices, convinced myself that doing something stupid was a good idea. There have been people in my life who I knew if I was around them, I was going to do things I should not do. I think Satan and his buddies were around poking me to make bad choices. The devil (Satan) is real, but today I know when he is poking me to make the wrong choice because Jesus is helping me.

PRAYER

Jesus, keep me strong in knowing that You and Your good heavenly warrior angels are stronger and will always win when I chose You. Jesus, help me remember to always bring my fears, choices, thoughts to You and not let Satan take them to places he wants me to go. I trust You, Jesus, with all my heart, my mind, and my soul. Amen

SCRIPTURE

James 4:7
"Submit yourselves therefore to God.
Resist the devil, and he will flee from you."

TRAILHEAD

Sometimes things happen, and we want to ask God why. The one thing you must know in your heart is that He loves you dearly. He gave up His son to die for you and me—that says everything. When you are scared or feel bad, it helps to say out loud, "Satan, get away from me. I belong to God. Jesus is my brother and He protects me with all the good heavenly warrior angels. Leave me alone." Amen! Write a note telling God thank you for protecting you, even in the small things.

TRAIL NOTES

DOING
(SOMETHING SPECIAL)

I remember my youngest son used to walk the neighbor's garbage cans all the way up her long, long driveway on Mondays when he was walking home from school. She didn't ask him to; he never told her or expected a thank you. He was just being kind. Those things, the things you do but don't expect money or a thank you, things you just do, are super powerful. We are called to help others and do good, and you know it is right because it feels so good inside.

PRAYER

Jesus, thank You for all the kind things that people do for me.
Thank You for my mom, my dad, my grandparents, (those who care for you).
Jesus, thank You for my teachers, my mentors, my friends.
I have been given a lot, Jesus, so help me be a doer too.

SCRIPTURE

Colossians 3:17

"And whatever you do, in word or deed, do everything in the name of the Lord Jesus, giving thanks to God the Father through him."

TRAILHEAD

God loves a giver. When we give by helping someone, it feels good deep inside. Think of some things people do for you like having your clothes washed, food at home, rides to places. Write down some things people do for you and some things you can do for others. Don't say anything or expect anything in return.

LAUGHING

In the movie *Elf*, Elf says "I like smiling, smiling is my favorite." That makes me laugh. I have laughed so hard it made me cry. I have one friend who always makes me laugh. It is so fun to be around him. Laughing can also hurt someone's feelings if we laugh at them when they are hurt. It is amazing that something that makes us feel so good can also make us feel so bad. I say laugh—we need funny jokes and best friends to laugh with. But be careful not to hurt someone's feelings. Always treat others the way you want to be treated. Now, smile!

PRAYER

Jesus, thank You for laughter and smiling. Jesus, help me to choose joy and laughter and not anger or being mean. Jesus, help me bring a smile to other people's face by saying nice things and doing nice things. Sometimes, Jesus, I want to be mad and angry; help me to choose to smile. Amen

SCRIPTURE

Psalm 126:2
"Then our mouth was filled with laughter, and our tongue with shouts of joy; then they said among the nations, 'The Lord has done great things for them.'"

TRAILHEAD

There are days we just don't want to smile. There are days laughing is not what we want to do. Think of something you always thought was funny, a dog dancing, a joke, a funny movie. Write down things that make you smile. When you are mad, try your best to think about the things that make you smile.
Make smiling your favorite.

DIVORCE

When my mom and dad divorced, I really don't remember having anything to say. I am sure I cried or was upset the family was going to be split, but I was just a kid, what did I know?

I don't like divorce, but there are times it is going to happen. You may be the one person a friend tells that their parents are getting a divorce. Be a good listener for your friend.

Parents are not perfect. Do your best to not be too hard on them, and if you have another adult—an uncle, aunt, coach, teacher, or mentor—tell them what is going on in your life. Share it with your best friends' parents. You never want to keep hard things to yourself.

You are not alone. Lots of your friends have been through divorce. You can make it through it.

PRAYER

Jesus, why are things like divorce even something that happens? I don't understand, Lord, but You do, and I have to trust You because this is hard. Lord, I pray for my friends whose parents are going through divorce or have divorced. Jesus, please help them feel safe and if I can help them, tell me the words and things I can do. I trust You, Jesus. Amen

SCRIPTURE

Exodus 14:14
"The Lord will fight for you, and you have only to be silent."

TRAILHEAD

You may not have parents who are divorced—thank Jesus. But you have friends who have divorced parents. Invite them to do things with you when you can. If your parents are split up, you are not alone, but you can make it through this. Write a note to God thanking Him for your parents being together or tell Him how you are feeling if they are not. He is here for you, He really is, and remember, it's NOT your fault.

KOZ PRAYER

Lord, thank You for making us strong and
fierce warriors for You. We hunt, we fish,
and we share our faith with others.
God bless our country. Amen

KOZ PLEDGE

"No KOZ Left Behind"

I solemnly pledge under oath that I will never
leave my KOZ brothers behind. I will always be kind
to them, help them when they look like they have
too much, run to them when they yell for help,
give them the best seat and first chance at everything.
They are my brothers; we fight evil together.

ABOUT THE AUTHOR

TJ Greaney is an award-winning outdoor travel and adventure writer, radio show host, and past President of the Texas Outdoor Writers Association. He is also founder of Kids Outdoor Zone (KOZ), a hunting, fishing, and outdoor adventure program for boys 8 to 18. He is passionate about teaching boys to become the men God has created them to be. He wants to let every young guy know they matter, they can "Do Hard Things," and no matter what has happened in the past or what anyone says, God really does care about them.

If you ask TJ his passions, he would tell you Jesus Christ, his family including dear friends, the ministry of KOZ, hunting, fishing, camping, and hiking mountains with his trusted dog, Hinge.

TJ and his wife, Sandra, have three adult children with amazing spouses, two granddaughters, one grandson, and more on the way! They live on a small farm in Smithville, Texas.

Made in the USA
Coppell, TX
13 April 2023